DECLINE AND RETURN TO MAINLINE STEAM

SPECIAL TRAINS IN THE 1960s, 1970s AND 1980s

LAURIE GOLDEN

AMBERLEY

First published 2024

Amberley Publishing
The Hill, Stroud
Gloucestershire, GL5 4EP

www.amberley-books.com

Copyright © Laurie Golden, 2024

The right of Laurie Golden to be identified as
the Author of this work has been asserted in
accordance with the Copyrights, Designs and
Patents Act 1988.

ISBN 978 1 3981 1909 3 (print)
ISBN 978 1 3981 1910 9 (ebook)

British Library Cataloguing in Publication Data.
A catalogue record for this book is available from
the British Library.

Origination by Amberley Publishing.
Printed in the UK.

Introduction

The images in this book, all scanned from colour slides, cover the period from when I started colour photography in 1963 to when I stopped still photography to concentrate on video recording in 1989. I actually started video recording in 1985, however, so from then to the end of 1989 my still photography was much reduced.

In this book, my main interpretation of 'special trains' is steam-hauled mainline rail tours organised for enthusiasts, but does not exclude trains arranged for other reasons that can be defined as 'special'. The book is arranged in three sections that cover the 1960s, 1970s and 1980s. Living in Surbiton during the 1960s, most of my activity was in the southern part of England, but as the period from 1963 to 1968 saw the increasingly rapid decline of mainline steam, my travels were forced to range further afield. Space does not allow exhaustive coverage of the rail tours I did photograph, so I have tried to make as varied a selection as possible. The images are arranged in chronological order throughout.

As the 1960s progressed, mainline steam was being progressively eliminated region by region. It was eliminated from the Western Region by the end of 1965, and the Southern Region in July 1967. As closures/withdrawals became imminent, there were an increasing number of special trains to mark 'last line' and 'last loco of class'. Regular steam on BR ceased on 4 August 1968, and in the dying months was concentrated entirely in the north-west of England.

The formal last day of steam on British Railways, on 4 August 1968, proved somewhat chaotic and a bit of a nightmare for both passengers and railway photographers. No less than six different rail tours had been organised, all travelling in various directions around an area between Manchester, Southport, Hellifield and Carnforth. The two trains originating from London were delayed by Sunday engineering works on the main line even before steam haulage commenced. These delays had a knock-on effect on schedules in the steam section, which in turn upset the timings of those trains originating in the local area. From a photographer's point of view, it took some organising in advance to try and see as many of these as possible, but the increasing delays totally upset these plans. Bear in mind that in those days there were no mobile phones or internet to instantly find out what was happening to the services. The rail tours were:

BR, 'Last Days of Steam'
No. 45305 Manchester, Wigan and Southport area.

GC Enterprises, 'Farewell to Steam'
No. 45156 Stockport–Manchester–Carnforth and return.

LCGB, 'Farewell to Steam'
Ex-London, various locos, Blackburn–Hellifield–Carnforth and return. It arrived back in London just after midnight, 2 hours late.

RCTS, 'End of Steam Commemorative'
Ex-London, Manchester, Rochdale, Blackburn, Hellifield, Skipton, Accrington area. Final arrival back in Euston was at 2.15 a.m. – 270 minutes late!

SLS, 'Farewell to Steam No. 1'
Nos 44871 and 44894, Manchester–Diggle–Huddersfield–Copy Pit–Wigan–Bootle–Manchester.

SLS, 'Farewell to Steam No. 2'
Nos 44874 and 45017, duplicate of No. 1, running approximately 30 minutes behind.

The very end of steam on the network was the BR-organised last day '15 Guinea Special' on Sunday 11 August. Thereafter, the only steam permitted on the network was ex-LNER A3 Class 4-6-2 No. 60103 *Flying Scotsman*. In 1963, Alan Pegler bought No. 60103 into preservation and restored it in LNER livery as No. 4472. His contract with British Railways allowed him to run the loco on the network until 31 December 1971. Consequently, it made a number of trips round the country up to and after August 1968 until its ill-fated trip to the USA in 1969.

At that time, hardly anyone expected to see steam on the main lines again. For instance, no one could have imagined being able to see a GWR King in 1983 on one of its old stamping grounds emerging from the Severn Tunnel (see p. 75). Or even leaving Paddington, as ex-GWR No. 6000 *King George V* did with some ceremony on 1 March 1979 (see p. 58).

However, in 1971, Peter Prior, managing director of Bulmers Cider in Hereford, proposed to Richard Marsh, the recently appointed chairman of the BR Board, that KGV might haul a train on a Bulmers promotional tour of the country. At this time, KGV was under the custodianship of Bulmers at Hereford, and in addition they owned five Pullman coaches, painted in Bulmers un-Pullman-like colours of green, white and red. In early October KGV made a four-day tour with the five Pullmans and three extra BR Mark 1 coaches: from Hereford via Swindon to Birmingham, then down to Kensington Olympia and back to Hereford in two stages via Swindon.

The success of this trip led to an initially limited return to mainline steam in June 1972 over a few selected routes with certain approved locomotives. As the decade progressed, the number of routes, locos and trips increased, so in 1975 the Steam Locomotive Operators' Association was formed to assist train operators wishing to run mainline steam in their negotiations with BR. Probably the most eagerly anticipated was the return to steam over the Settle & Carlisle line in 1978. In the 1980s British Railways themselves organised repeat runs in the summer high season over certain routes, such as the Scarborough Spa and Cumbrian Mountain expresses.

The 150th anniversary celebrations of Rail 150 at Shildon in 1975 and Rocket 150 at Rainhill in 1980 lead to a number of interesting train movements, and the restoration of museum pieces that would not normally have been expected. Then came 'GWR 150' in 1985, which opened up the West Country to GWR steam.

Abbreviations

6000LA	6000 Locomotive Association
ARES	Altrinchamian Railway Excursion Society
BR	British Railways
GC	Great Central Railway
GMRS	Gainsborough Model Railway Society
GWR	Great Western Railway
GWS	Great Western Society

LCGB	Locomotive Club of Great Britain
LMS	London Midland & Scottish Railway
LNER	London & North Eastern Railway
LNWR	London & North Western Railway
LSWR	London & South Western Railway
HRCS	Home Counties Railway Society
HSE	Health & Safety Executive
M&GN	Midland & Great Northern Railway
MNLPS	Merchant Navy Locomotive Preservation Society
MR	Midland Railway
NB	North British Railway
RCTS	Railway Correspondence & Travel Society
SDJR	Somerset & Dorset Joint Railway
SLOA	Steam Locomotive Operators Association
SLS	Stephenson Locomotive Society
SR	Southern Railway
SRPS	Scottish Railway Preservation Society
WRS	Warwickshire Railway Society

1963–69

On 15 September 1963, a unique combination of locomotives passed through Wandsworth Common on the London–Brighton main line. Ex-Caledonian Railway 4-2-2 123 plus ex-LSWR T9 Class 4-4-0 120 hauled the 'Blue Belle' from Victoria to Haywards Heath, where Bluebell Railway motive power took the train to Horstead Keynes and Sheffield Park.

Meanwhile, 123 and 120 ran light engine to Brighton shed for turning and servicing before returning to Haywards Heath, where they posed in this position waiting for the train to return from Horstead Keynes.

Both engines were designed by Dugald Drummond, the unique 'single' 123 in 1886 while he was chief engineer for the Caledonian Railway, and 120 in 1899 after he had moved to the LSWR. The profile of 120 was changed by Urie in 1922, so a direct comparison of the original designs is not possible. 123 was withdrawn for preservation in 1935, while 120 had recently been withdrawn from regular service and painted in LSWR colours for occasional use on service and special trains.

Ex-LSWR S15 Class 4-6-0 heads the 'Hayling Farewell' on 3 November 1963 on the approach to Fratton. As the name suggests, this was a special train run to Havant and Hayling Island on the last day of operation of the Hayling Island branch. This engine hauled the first leg of the trip from Waterloo to Fratton, before being replaced for the journey to Havant.

Ex-LSWR M7 Class 0-4-4T No. 30053 is passing through Chipstead on the Tattenham Corner branch on 5 July 1964. The LCGB 'Surrey Wanderer' did precisely that, touring many lines in the area. No. 30053 initially hauled the train from Waterloo to Shepperton, then after picking up the train again at Purley wandered around the southern suburbs of London before finally ending up at Victoria. No. 30053 had already been withdrawn from regular service but can still be seen today on the Swanage Railway.

Ex-BR Class 3MT 2-6-2T stands at Winchester Chesil station on 6 September 1964 with the LCGB 'Anton & Test Valley' rail tour. Starting from here, it made a return trip via Southampton, Romsey and Andover to Ludgershall. By this time, the Didcot, Newbury & Southampton Railway had closed north of this point. The site is now a car park with the tunnel remains sealed off, but it is open for occasional visitors.

On 12 September 1964, Alan Pegler's 'Farnborough Flyer' hauled by ex-LNER A3 Class 4-6-2 No. 4472 *Flying Scotsman* approaches Basingstoke on the link from Western region at Reading West. It had travelled from Sheffield via Banbury. Southern motive power took the train on to Farnborough. The Farnborough International Airshow was (and still is) a biennial event displaying new civilian and military aircraft and associated technology.

Ex-SR S15 Class 4-6-0 No. 30839 is approaching Virginia Water on the line from Waterloo via Ascot on 18 October 1964. The train is the joint RCTS/LCGB 'Midhurst Belle'. No. 30839 is one of the Maunsell modified versions of the original Urie design of mixed traffic engines pictured in a previous image. It took the train as far as Woking.

At Woking, ex-SR USA Class 0-6-0T No. 30064 took the train via Guildford and Baynards to Christ's Hospital. It is pictured here near Worplesdon on the line to Guildford. The USA tanks were a wartime US Army Transportation Corps design, purchased by the SR in 1946. Designed for shunting, they were rarely seen on passenger-train duty, and spent a lot of their time in Southampton Docks.

Apart from the travel around parts of Surrey and Sussex, the primary object of the RCTS/LCGB tour was to make a final revenue-earning trip to Midhurst before the branch from Pulborough was lifted. Ex-SR Q Class 0-6-0 No. 30530 is here seen passing Selham on the return from Midhurst to Pulborough. Midhurst once had branches from the east, west and south, but closed to passengers in 1955. The branch from Pulborough in the east remained open for freight until closure on the day of this trip.

No. 30530 was used again later in the day to haul the train from Brighton to Kemp Town and return. Kemp Town is a suburb of Brighton, and this branch line was opened in 1869. Passenger services ceased in 1932, but the branch remained open for freight until 1971. The line featured a viaduct and a tunnel, the latter of which is being approached in this picture.

The next two images do not represent a railway enthusiast 'special' train, but it is a special train nonetheless. It is the special train to convey the body of Sir Winston Churchill for burial at Blaidon, near Blenheim Palace, on 30 January 1965. The appropriate locomotive to haul this train, ex-SR BB Class 4-6-2 No. 34051 *Winston Churchill*, is here at Nine Elms shed after preparation for the journey.

In very dismal weather conditions, No. 34051 is hauling the funeral train through Vauxhall station en route from Waterloo to Handborough. On the Southern Region, the disc headcodes normally indicated the train's route, but here it represents the sign synonymous with Sir Winston's wartime activities. His body is conveyed in the second vehicle, a bogie van specially painted in Pullman colours.

Southern engines on 'foreign' territory. U Class 2-6-0 No. 31639 pilots Q1 Class 0-6-0 No. 33006 near Kineton on the former Stratford-upon-Avon & Midland Junction Railway between Fenny Compton and Stratford. This HCRS 'Six Counties Railtour' from and to Paddington, reaching Warwick, Rugby, Wellingborough and Bedford, was hauled throughout by this combination. On 7 March 1965 there are remnants of an earlier snowfall.

From all the heads out of the windows, you would think that train M48 was an enthusiast special. In essence, it probably turned out to be thus, but it was in fact the last regular scheduled steam-hauled train to leave Paddington, the 4.15 p.m. Friday-only semi-fast to Banbury via Bicester on 11 June 1965. It is hauled by ex-BR Castle Class 4-6-0 No. 7029 *Clun Castle* passing Ardley. Although perpetuating the basic Collett design of 1923, it was actually constructed under the auspices of British Railways in 1950.

Ex-GWR Castle Class 4-6-0 No. 4079 *Pendennis Castle* is travelling at speed on the main line at the site of the former Goring water troughs on 8 August 1965 with a special train organised by book publisher Ian Allan. The train ran from Paddington to Worcester, out via Oxford and returned as here via Swindon. By this time No. 4079 was already in private ownership. After restoration it was back making special runs on the main line.

Ex-GWR 2800 Class 2-8-0 No. 3863 is passing through Wantage Road station on 15 August 1965 with the LCGB-organised 'Western Ranger', which, having set out from Waterloo, ran via Reading to visit Swindon Works and tour various branch lines in Wiltshire and Oxfordshire. No. 3863 was a Collett development of Churchward's 2800 Class, the GWR's main heavy freight locomotives.

Later the same day, ex-GWR 6100 Class 2-6-2T No. 6126 is passing Islip with the 'Western Ranger', returning from Bicester NW. This was part of the LNWR line running from Cambridge via Bedford and Bletchley to Oxford. Passenger services on this line were withdrawn in 1968, but there are plans to fully reopen this rail link. Collett's 6100 Class was introduced in 1931 for work in the London suburban area.

Ex-GWR Castle Class 4-6-0 No. 7029 *Clun Castle* is near Bramley on the line from Reading West to Basingstoke with the Warwickshire Railway Society's 'Hants & Dorset' rail tour on 5 September 1965. The tour ran from Birmingham via Reading and Eastleigh to Weymouth, and back to Birmingham via Westbury. No. 7029 worked the Banbury to Basingstoke and Weymouth to Banbury portions.

Ex-SR WC Class 4-6-2 No. 34002 *Salisbury* is viewed on the LCGB 'Vectis Farewell' tour near Billingshurst, on the line from Horsham to Littlehampton, on 3 October 1965. The participants toured the Isle of Wight lines, but the tour turned out to be somewhat of a misnomer, since the anticipated closure on that date of the Shanklin–Ventnor and Cowes lines was postponed until 1966.

On 17 October 1965, the 'GWR Cavalcade' was organised to move ex-GWR 1400 Class 0-4-2T 1420 and ex-GWR 6400 Class 0-6-0PT No. 6435 towards the Dart Valley Railway. These two locos came on the train at Worcester, and it is seen here near Cheltenham.

No. 1420 was removed from the train at Gloucester and the train continued down the former Midland line to Bristol with No. 6435 piloting ex-BR Castle Class 4-6-0 No. 7029 *Clun Castle*. It is pictured here near Charfield. The train returned to Birmingham with No. 7029 alone. No. 7029 itself was withdrawn from BR service at the end of the year.

Ex-LNER A4 Class 4-6-2 No. 60007 *Sir Nigel Gresley* is passing through Beaconsfield on 23 October 1965 with the A4 Preservation Society's 'Paddington Streamliner' rail tour. As the title indicates, the train was worked throughout into Paddington from Manchester via Birmingham Snow Hill. This train was run by the society to raise funds for No. 60007's preservation after it was withdrawn from BR service early in 1966.

Ex-SR S15 Class 4-6-0 No. 30837 is climbing the 1 in 80 through Liss Forest on the last leg to Waterloo of the 'S15 Commemorative' rail tour on 16 January 1966. This tour was organised to mark the withdrawal from service of the last S15s and was the final run of this loco. The tour was so over-subscribed that a second train had to be run the week before for the later subscribers.

On 27 February 1966, the LCGB organised the 'Dorset Belle' rail tour from Waterloo to visit the Swanage branch, Weymouth and the former GWR branch from Maiden Newton to Bridport. Passing through the tiny station at Toller Porcorum, the train is heading for Bridport being top and tailed by two ex-LMS 2MT 2-6-2Ts, Nos 41284 and 41301.

Another tour organised by the A4 Preservation Society, this time on Southern Region metals. Ex-LNER A4 Class 4-6-2 No. 60024 *Kingfisher* hauled the 'Victory' rail tour from Waterloo to Weymouth, and back via Yeovil and Salisbury. It is here approaching the summit of the 1 in 80 bank from Sherborne to Milborne Port.

The RCTS organised two tours to visit the Longmoor Military Railway in April 1966. Two weeks earlier the tour had run in awful weather, but on 30 April the sun shone on ex-SR U Class 2-6-0s Nos 31791 and 31639 near Byfleet as they take the train from Waterloo to Woking. No. 31791 was rebuilt as U Class from Maunsell's River Class 2-6-4T *River Adur* in 1928.

A unique feature of these Longmoor trips was the use of Military Railway's 2-10-0 WD600 *Gordon* on Southern Railway lines. It worked the train down the Portsmouth line from Woking to Liss, then after various runs with other military locos on the Military Railway, *Gordon* hauled the special from Bordon via Ash Vale and Ascot to Staines. It is seen here between Ash Vale and Frimley.

Ex-LNER A2 Class 4-6-2 No. 60532 *Blue Peter* was brought down specially from Scotland for this LCGB A2 Commemorative rail tour from Waterloo to Exeter via Honiton, returning via Westbury and Salisbury. The date was 14 August 1966. No. 60532's performance was far from auspicious: it stalled on Honiton bank and is here seen just pulling away from the enforced stop.

On 27 August 1966, the Railway Society of Scotland organised a rail tour around the suburbs of Edinburgh using ex-NB 1888-designed Class J36 0-6-0 No. 65345. On a dull grey day, it here seen arriving for a photographic stop at Blackford Hill station, en route on the former NB line from Smeaton to Slateford.

After returning from a visit to North Leith, No. 65345 is on the final leg of its journey to Edinburgh Waverley, crossing the viaduct over the Water of Leith at Slateford.

On 3 September 1966, the former GC Main Line from Nottingham Victoria to Marylebone closed as a through route. To mark the occasion the LCGB organised the Great Central rail tour, with ex-SR MN Class 4-6-2 No. 35030 *Elder Dempster Lines* working from Waterloo up the GC line to Nottingham. After touring other GC lines in the Midlands No. 35030 worked the train back to Marylebone, seen here near Rugby.

Organised by the Gainsborough Model Railway Society, the 'Farnborough Flyer' of 10 September 1966 was again hauled by A3 4-6-2 No. 4472 *Flying Scotsman*. The route from Doncaster took it via the Midland Main Line, Acton Wells Junction and Feltham right through to Farnborough. It is here passing Virginia Water before joining the Southern Main Line at Byfleet.

On 17 September 1966, ex-GWR Manor Class 4-6-0 No. 7808 *Cookham Manor* is passing through Gerrards Cross with a special train from Birmingham Snow Hill organised by the Reading Group of the Great Western Society to visit their open day at Taplow. At that time, the group had a base at Taplow goods shed and a number of their locos were on display.

Earlier on 17 September 1966, No. 4472 *Flying Scotsman* had worked the Locomotive Preservation (Sussex) Ltd 'Flying Scotsman Goes South' from Victoria to Brighton, then on to Eastleigh. It is passing through Streatham Common, undoubtedly on Southern territory as it passes 2 HAL unit No. 2625. I wonder what the HSE would think today about the lineside trespass!

Later, on 17 September, the Flying Scotsman trip was worked from Eastleigh to Salisbury and back by two cx-BR 4MT 2-6-4Ts, Nos 80152 and 80016. This shows the return near Romsey, before No. 4472 worked the train back to Victoria.

Two un-rebuilt Bulleid Pacifics double-heading was always enough to spark interest, particularly if working on the 'new line' from Surbiton via Claygate to Guildford, which rarely saw steam activity. On 16 October 1966, the LCGB 'Dorset & Hants' rail tour took this route to Havant, Fareham and Bournemouth. No. 34019 *Bideford* and No. 34023 *Blackmore Vale* are near Cobham.

Entering the last year of steam on the Southern, this combination of locos was becoming more popular. Un-rebuilt Bulleid Pacifics No. 34102 *Lapford* and No. 34057 *Biggin Hill* are crossing the viaduct over the Bourne tributary to the River Test at Hurstbourne on 22 January 1967. The train is the LCGB 'Bridport Belle' rail tour, which ran to Maiden Newton via Salisbury and Westbury.

On 5 February 1967, the LCGB ran their 100th tour, the 'South Western Suburban' rail tour. As the name suggests, it visited various suburban branches, including Chessington and Shepperton, with a range of motive power. The section from Windsor & Eton Riverside to Staines was worked by ex-SR WC Class 4-6-2 No. 34100 *Appledore*, seen here crossing the River Thames just after leaving Windsor.

On 4 March 1967, Ian Allan ran two steam-hauled specials to commemorate the last through working from Paddington to Birkenhead. The second of these, named 'The Zulu', was worked by ex-BR Castle Class 4-6-0 No. 7029 *Clun Castle* from Banbury to Chester. After the train had been taken to Birkenhead, it worked it back from Chester to Birmingham. It is seen here leaving Banbury.

Ex-LNER K4 Class 2-6-0 *The Great Marquess* was bought from BR by Viscount Garnock and returned to LNER livery as No. 3442. It hauled various rail tours from May 1963 and was brought down to the Southern for this Locomotive Preservation (Sussex) Ltd's 'The Marquess Goes South South West' from Victoria to Brighton, Chichester and Southampton on 12 March 1967. It is pictured climbing the 1 in 64 Grosvenor bank out of Victoria.

Steam on the London–Brighton main line was rare at the best of times, yet only a week later, on 19 March 1967, rebuilt ex-BR WC Class 4-6-2 No. 34108 *Wincanton* is crossing the impressive Ouse Valley Viaduct just north of Haywards Heath on the last leg from Eastbourne to Victoria of the Southern Counties Touring Society's Southern Rambler tour, advertised as the last steam train to Brighton and Eastbourne.

The RCTS organised the 'Wrexham, Mold & Connah's Quay Railway' rail tour on 29 April 1967. The yellow gorse makes a colourful background as it is leaving Rhydymwyn on the Denbigh–Mold line with Stanier's two-cylinder version of the ex-LMS 4MT 2-6-4Ts Nos 42616 and 42647, heading for Wrexham Exchange station.

Wrexham Central station was listed for closure in the Beeching Report but was retained due to its closeness to the city centre. The RCTS rail tour of 29 April 1967 is pictured here after it was hauled the short distance from Wrexham Exchange by ex-LMS 8F 2-8-0 No. 48697.

No. 4472 *Flying Scotsman* is passing Thetford on 20 May 1967 with the Gainsborough Model Railway Society's 'Norfolkman' rail tour from King's Cross via Hitchen and Cambridge to Norwich. It was the first steam-hauled passenger train into Norwich since the 1950s.

After the passengers had the chance of a motor-launch trip on the River Bure, No. 4472 is making a very smoky departure from Norwich Thorpe station. Note that No. 4472 now has the second tender, which was acquired by Alan Pegler in 1966 to enable greater distances to be travelled between stops as water troughs were being removed.

As the 9 July end of Southern steam was rapidly approaching, there were a number of rail tours being arranged. On 11 June 1967 the WRS organised the 'Farewell to Steam on the L.S.W.R.' rail tour from Birmingham to Swanage and Weymouth using a variety of motive power. The return leg from Salisbury to Basingstoke is here passing through Porton hauled by ex-SR WC 4-6-2 No. 34023 *Blackmore Vale*.

The following week, on 18 June 1967, the RCTS organised the last privately sponsored rail tour on the Southern – 'Farewell to Southern Steam'. The tour again used the 'new line' between Surbiton and Guildford, then via Havant to Bournemouth and Weymouth, with a last run down the Swanage Branch. It is here actually crossing the junction with the Leatherhead line at Effingham with ex-BR 5MT 4-6-0 Nos 73029 and 34023 *Blackmore Vale* on the outward leg.

On 18 November 1967, the ARES ran 'The Palatine' to Stoke-on-Trent, Stockport and Sheffield. No. 4472 *Flying Scotsman* hauled the train from St Pancras to the Leicester area down the Midland Main Line, and back from Sheffield to King's Cross. Early morning autumn sunshine illuminates the train at Scratchwood, soon after leaving St Pancras. This is now the site of the M1 Scratchwood service area.

By 1968, the only steam in the London area was No. 4472 *Flying Scotsman*. On 9 June 1968, the Gainsborough Model Railway Society ran the 'Stapleford Park' rail tour from King's Cross to Grantham to visit the Miniature Railway and Lion Reserve at the Park. No. 4472 hauled the train throughout, and is here seen leaving the London terminus, still using the second tender.

Now nearing the end of BR steam, 21 July 1968 saw the Roch Valley Railway Society's 'Manchester–Southport Steam Excursions'. Ex-LMS Class 5MT 4-6-0 No. 44888 is crossing Sankey Viaduct, near Newton-le-Willows, with the first leg of the trip from Manchester on the former LNW line to Liverpool. This viaduct is a Grade I listed building, constructed in 1830, the earliest major viaduct in the world.

The declared purpose of the Roch Valley tour on 21 July 1968 was to travel between Manchester and Southport by four different routes. The third leg was a rather more convoluted route via Rochdale, Copy Pit and Blackburn, hauled in this instance by ex-BR Britannia Class 4-6-2 No. 70013 *Oliver Cromwell*. It is seen crossing Lydgate Viaduct, on the 1 in 65 climb from Todmorden to Copy Pit summit.

On 28 July 1968, the joint Manchester Rail Travel Society/Severn Valley Railway Society 'Farewell to BR Steam' rail tour ran from Birmingham to tour the Manchester, Skipton and Carnforth area. Ex-LMS 5MT 4-6-0s Nos 45073 and 45156 *Ayrshire Yeomanry* are crossing Entwhistle Viaduct on the line between Bolton and Blackburn. No. 45156 was one of only four LMS Class 5MTs to be named.

On the 28 July tour, at Rose Grove, ex-LMS Class 8F No. 48773 took over the train for the leg via Rochdale and Bolton to Manchester Victoria, where modern traction took over for the return to Birmingham. No. 48773 has just emerged from the tunnel on the 1 in 70 approach to Copy Pit summit.

I, with my late colleagues Bill Sumner and John Scrase, planned to photograph at Arnside the last steam working from Barrow-in-Furness, the 8.30 p.m. parcels train to Carnforth, booking specially into a hotel overlooking the water and viaduct with the hope of a sunset. It was a calculated risk as it all had to be booked in advance. This was the outcome, with ex-LMS Class 5MT 4-6-0 No. 44781 crossing Kent Viaduct.

In the introduction, I explained the complexities of photographing the group of special trains run on 4 August 1968. Starting from Manchester before the schedules began to disintegrate, ex-LMS Class 5MT 4-6-0 No. 45156 *Ayrshire Yeomanry* is crossing Entwhistle Viaduct with the GC Enterprises train heading from Bolton to Blackburn.

By now running around 45 minutes late, the LCGB 'Farewell to Steam' is crossing Entwhistle Viaduct heading from Bolton to Blackburn hauled by ex-BR Britannia Class 4-6-2 No. 70013 *Oliver Cromwell* and ex-LMS Class 5MT 4-6-0 No. 44781. No. 70013 was the one remaining Britannia still in service, all others having been withdrawn at the end of 1967.

It took a quick walk up the hill to get in position for the second SLS 'Farewell to Steam' special which crossed Entwhistle Viaduct in the opposite direction some 55 minutes later, hauled by ex-LMS Class 5MT 4-6-0s Nos 44874 and 45017. There is considerable lineside trespass on the other side of the viaduct.

On Sunday 11 August, to make a finale to steam, BR ran the now famous '15 Guinea Special' from Liverpool via Manchester to Carlisle and return. Ex-BR Britannia Class 4-6-2 No. 70013 *Oliver Cromwell* hauled the train over the Settle & Carlisle line, here seen crossing Moorcock Viaduct just north of Garsdale on the approach to a photographic stop at Ais Gill.

This picture was taken looking towards Ais Gill minutes after the train had passed. Never would this amount have traffic been seen in this remote countryside. With Ais Gill a couple of miles away, cars have been parked on both sides of the road. This left just enough room for a single track of cars. The resulting jam, when streams of cars travelling in opposite directions met midway, apparently took hours to resolve.

After the farewells to steam in August 1968, No. 4472 *Flying Scotsman* was the only steam loco left running on BR lines, but in 1969 Alan Pegler arranged for the loco to tour the USA. This formal send-off took place at Twickenham on 21 August 1969 because modifications to the coaching stock had been carried out here. A bell has already been fitted to the front of No. 4472.

1970–79

On 7 October 1971, ex-GWR King Class 4-6-0 No. 6000 *King George V* is passing through Sonning Cutting, near Twyford, with the third day of HP Bulmers Ltd's four-day inaugural 'Return to Steam'. Running just between Kensington Olympia and Swindon, the train is formed of the five Pullman coaches owned by Bulmers (in rather uncharacteristic livery) plus three Mark 1s.

On 1 October 1972, the Great Western Society ran a return trip from Didcot to Tyseley using ex-GWR Modified Hall Class 4-6-0 No. 6998 *Burton Agnes Hall*, seen here approaching Culham on the outward leg. The GWS moved into the redundant engine shed at Didcot in 1967, and at roughly the same time Patrick Whitehouse had established a base at the former depot at Tyseley.

On 14 October 1972, ex-LMS Jubilee Class 4-6-0 No. 5596 *Bahamas* is nearing the summit of the 1 in 100 bank to Church Stretton with the SLS/Bahamas Locomotive Society's 'Welsh Marches' rail tour. No. 5596 worked between Shrewsbury and Hereford, where No. 6000 *King George V* took over for the run to Newport. On the same day, the LCGB organised a tour to return the locos in the opposite direction.

The late Trevor Owen and I learned that No. 6000 *King George V* was spending much of 11 November 1972 filming from Hereford to Newport and back with the five Bulmers Pullmans, which gave opportunities for a number of shots along the route. No. 6000 is here on a filming run past approaching Abergavenny station.

Returning from Newport, the low 11 November sunshine highlights No. 6000 *King George V* as it passes Ponthir, near Caerleon. The chimneys of the Star Brickworks are a local landmark. The Pullman cars, owned by Bulmers, are painted in their own green and red livery and carry Hereford's coat of arms.

Bringing the photographic day of 11 November 1972 to a close, No. 6000 *King George V* passes the site of Tram Inn station, around 5 miles south of Hereford, illuminated by the late afternoon sunshine. The station, which closed in 1964, was named after a local public house which in turn was named after a tramway that carried coal into Hereford before the advent of the railway.

The Great Western Society ran the 'Great Western Returns' on 24 June 1973. Ex-GWR Modified Hall Class 4-6-0 *Burton Agnes Hall* is passing through Culham station having just left Didcot with the opening steam leg to Hereford via Worcester.

From Hereford on 24 June, the GWS 'Great Western Returns' was taken to Shrewsbury by ex-GWR King Class 4-6-0 No. 6000 *King George V*. It is seen here with the return to Hereford near the summit of the 1 in 100 bank at Church Stretton. Two of the Bulmers Pullmans are attached to the stock.

On 1 July 1973, the LCGB ran two 'Gresley Commemorative' rail tours from Euston to Birmingham and then steam hauled from Tyseley to Didcot and return. Ex-LNER V2 Class 2-6-0 No. 4771 (BR 60800) *Green Arrow* passes Fenny Compton, north of Banbury. No. 4771, part of the National Collection, had recently been restored to working order.

A little over an hour later on 1 July, the second LCGB 'Gresley Commemorative' trip passes Fenny Compton headed by ex-LNER A4 Class 4-6-2 No. 4498 (BR 60007) *Sir Nigel Gresley*. The truncated line in the foreground was part of the former Stratford-upon-Avon & Midland Junction Railway route to Northampton and Bedford.

A GWR King and an LNER A3 double-heading was surely unique when, on 22 September 1973, No. 6000 *King George V* and No. 4472 *Flying Scotsman* head north through Bromfield, north of Ludlow. The train is the 6000 Locomotive Association-arranged 'Atlantic Venturers Express' from Plymouth to Shrewsbury via Newport. No. 4472 plus the five Bulmers Pullmans headed north on a fourteen-day tour with the cider train around Northern England, while 6000 returned the main train to Newport.

The Didcot Railway Centre held an open day on 27 October 1973. A rail tour from Manchester was hauled between Tyseley and Didcot by No. 4472 *Flying Scotsman* for it to be displayed there. It is seen here returning to Tyseley at Culham in the evening, just after leaving Didcot.

Ex-GWR Castle Class 4-6-0 No. 4079 *Pendennis Castle* was one of the locos approved for mainline running when the BR ban on steam was lifted. On 6 April 1974, two steam specials were organised by Flying Scotsman Enterprises. 'The Great Northern', from Northampton via Kensington Olympia, ran from Newport to Shrewsbury hauled by No. 4079, seen here passing Marshbrook on the northbound climb to Church Stretton.

The other trip on 6 April 1974, 'The Great Western', ran from Swansea to Newport and again up to Shrewsbury. No. 4472 *Flying Scotsman* hauled the train to Shrewsbury, then No. 4079 *Pendennis Castle* returned the train to Newport, here approaching Church Stretton. No. 4472 returned 'The Great Northern' to Newport.

Three days later on 9 April 1974, No. 4079 *Pendennis Castle* ran a rail tour from Newport via Chepstow, Gloucester and Stratford-upon-Avon to Birmingham. It is seen here passing under the aqueduct carrying the Stratford-upon-Avon Canal at Bearley Cross, near Wilmcote.

The Merchant Navy Preservation Society organised 'Return to Steam No. 3' for ex-SR MN Class 4-6-2 No. 35028 *Clan Line*, which had recently been returned to service to run in preservation. The train ran from London via Swindon and Bristol to Hereford, where No. 35028 took over for the run to Shrewsbury and Chester. It is crossing the River Dee on Newbridge Viaduct, just south of Ruabon.

The return working of the MNPS 'Return to Steam No. 3' was returned south by ex-GWR King Class 4-6-2 No. 6000 *King George V*, again seen crossing Newbridge Viaduct. Also on 26 April 1975, the M&GN Joint Railway Society Ltd ran the 'Mayflower' from London via Birmingham and Worcester to Hereford and again through to Chester, using Nos 6000 and 35028 in the opposite directions.

The Great Western Society ran a special train from Didcot via Evesham and Worcester to visit the Bulmers site at Hereford on 14 June 1975. It was hauled throughout by ex-GWR Manor Class 4-6-0 No. 7808 *Cookham Manor* and ex-GWR Modified Hall Class 4-6-0 No. 6998 *Burton Agnes Hall*. It is here crossing Ledbury Viaduct on the line through Malvern to Hereford.

No. 7808 *Cookham Manor* leads No. 6998 *Burton Agnes Hall* near Moreton-in-Marsh, between Evesham and Oxford, with the return GWS special from Hereford to Didcot. The train is formed of the GWS-preserved Great Western set of coaches.

On 18 August 1975, ex-GWR Manor Class 4-6-0 No. 7808 *Cookham Manor* is crossing Yarm Viaduct approaching Stockton with four GWR coaches en route to Rail 150 at Shildon. Approximately thirty steam locos were on display in the wagon works from 24–30 August, followed on the 31st by a steam cavalcade from Shildon to Heighington. It marked the 150th anniversary of the opening of the Stockton & Darlington Railway.

The Wirral Railway Society ran the 'North Eastern' on 21 September 1975 from Liverpool via Shefield and York to Newcastle. Ex-LNER B1 Class 4-6-0 No. 1306 *Mayflower* and A3 Class 4-6-2 No. 4472 *Flying Scotsman* hauled the train from York to Newcastle and back, seen here between Northallerton and Darlington. 'Mayflower' was the name carried by No. 61379, not No. 61306, in BR days.

On 4 October 1975, the Bahamas Locomotive Society ran the 'Welsh Borderer' from Manchester to Didcot via Chester and Hereford. Ex-LMS Jubilee Class 4-6-0 No. 5690 *Leander* is crossing Chirk Viaduct en route from Chester to Shrewsbury. The aqueduct carrying the Shropshire Union Canal is in the foreground.

On 17 April 1976, ex-BR Castle Class 4-6-0 No. 7029 *Clun Castle* hauled the 'Shakespeare Don' from Birmingham to Stratford-upon-Avon then via Oxford to Didcot, viewed here just south of Oxford.

Viewed from the grounds of the castle at Knaresborough, we see ex-LNWR Precedent Class 2-4-0 No. 790 *Hardwicke* and ex-MR Compound 4-4-0 No. 1000 crossing the viaduct over the River Nidd. They are hauling the GMRS 'London & North Western & Midland Railways Joint Tour' from York via Knaresborough to Leeds, then on to Carnforth on 24 April 1976.

Ex-LNWR No. 790 *Hardwicke* and Midland Compound No. 1000 are near Long Preston on the approach to Settle Junction on their way to Carnforth with the GMRS trip of 24 April 1976. Both locos had been restored to working order for Rail 150 and had gained mainline certification for running occasional rail tours.

Ex-GWR Modified Hall Class 4-6-0 No. 6998 *Burton Agnes Hall* and ex-GWR Hall Class 4-6-0 No. 5900 *Hinderton Hall* are approaching Fenny Compton with the Great Western Society vintage coaches on the return to Didcot with a trip the society had organised from Didcot to Dorridge on 15 May 1976.

On 15 May 1976, No. 6998 *Burton Agnes Hall* pilots No. 5900 *Hinderton Hall* on the approach to Banbury with the return of the GWS trip from Dorridge to Banbury. Both locos are preserved at Didcot and currently await overhaul. This view clearly shows the Hawksworth and Collett design of tenders.

An unlikely motive power combination for the 6000 Locomotive Association 'The Merchant Venturer & The Lakelander' rail tour on 22 May 1976 is ex-LNER B1 Class 4-6-0 No. 1306 *Mayflower* and ex-LNER A3 Class 4-6-2 No. 4472 *Flying Scotsman*. The pair make a volcanic departure from Ravenglass for Sellafield, having dropped off passengers to visit the Ravenglass & Eskdale Railway.

On 22 May 1976, after turning at Sellafield and having picked up their passengers at Ravenglass, No. 1306 *Mayflower* and No. 4472 *Flying Scotsman* accelerate across the viaduct over the River Esk at Eskmeals. The tour originated at Bristol and travelled via Birmingham and Stafford and up the West Coast Main Line to Carnforth.

On 23 May 1976, ex-LNWR Precedent Class 2-4-0 No. 790 *Hardwicke* made four return trips from Carnforth to Grange-over-Sands hauling four coaches unassisted. The trips were called 'The North Western'. It is here crossing the Kent Viaduct at Arnside with the second run from Carnforth.

Before the third run of No. 790 *Hardwicke* on 23 May 1976, the loco was turned at Carnforth. It is now shown returning to Carnforth and passing through Silverdale station. Hardwicke's claim to fame occurred in August 1895 when it took 2 hours and 6 minutes for the 141 miles from Crewe to Carlisle, with an average speed of 67.1 mph and a top speed of over 90 mph, setting up a new speed record during the Race to the North.

On 23 May 1976, No. 790 *Hardwicke* is crossing the inlet to Leighton Moss at Crag Foot to the total oblivion of two youngsters fishing in the brook. Hardwicke was withdrawn from service in 1932 and stored in Crewe Works until it was moved to Clapham Museum in 1962. On closure of the museum in 1974, it was moved to Carnforth where it was restored to working order for Rail 150.

On 19 June 1976, No. 790 *Hardwicke* was moved to York by a pairing that I can only describe as 'little and large'. It is piloting ex-BR Class 9F 2-10-0 No. 92220 *Evening Star* over the viaduct at Clapham with Ingleborough peak prominent in the background. The amount of assistance it was giving to the 9F is open to conjecture.

The 'Fells and Dales Railtour' from Carnforth to York on 19 June 1976 was organised by the LCGB. Originating at Crewe, the route to York took it via Leeds and then the loop to York via Harrogate. No. 790 *Hardwicke* and No. 92220 *Evening Star* are crossing the viaduct over the River Crimple on the southern outskirts of the town. This Grade II listed structure has thirty-one arches.

Into 1977, on 3 April, ex-BR Castle Class 4-6-0 No. 7029 *Clun Castle* is working the *Coventry Evening Telegraph* 'Midland Wightsman' en route from Birmingham to Leamington Spa, seen near Hatton. This was the second return working to Leamington Spa that day.

On 23 April 1977, two steam-hauled trips ran between Hereford and Chester: operated turn about by No. 6000 *King George V* and ex-LMS Princess Royal Class 4-6-2 No. 6201 *Princess Elizabeth*. No. 6201 is climbing the 1 in 72 at Gresford Colliery with the 'Severn Valley Limited'. Gresford Colliery closed in 1973 but was the site of one of Britain's worst colliery disasters in 1934 when 266 men died.

On 1 May 1977, ex-LNER A4 Class 4-6-2 No. 4498 *Sir Nigel Gresley* was transferred to its new working base at Steamtown Carnforth after completion of overhaul. No. 4498 just catches the sunshine at Gigglewick as it climbs the 1 in 100 from Settle Junction on the last leg of the special train from York via Leeds.

SLOA operated the 'Great Western Envoy' on 29 May 1977 from Euston to Didcot via Birmingham and Banbury. This was the final rail tour using ex-GWR Castle Class 4-6-0 No. 4079 *Pendennis Castle* before its move to Australia. No. 4079 worked the train from the Birmingham area to Didcot and back, and is seen here near Tackley on the southbound run.

On the following day, No. 4079 *Pendennis Castle* worked down from Tyseley to Avonmouth Docks, near Bristol, to load on ship for the journey to Australia. No. 4079 is nearing the end of its rail journey as it works along the branch to Avonmouth. It had been sold to the Hamersley Iron Company based in Western Australia. It remained there until 2000, when it was offered back and returned to the GWS.

On 25 June 1977, ex-BR Castle Class 4-6-0 No. 7029 *Clun Castle* worked the 'Western Cavalier' from Saltley to Newport via Didcot and is seen here near Radley. The train had run diesel hauled to Birmingham from London. No. 35028 *Clan Line* took over from No. 7029 at Newport for the run to Hereford.

Sunshine highlights ex-SR MN Class 4-6-2 No. 35028 *Clan Line* against a stormy background as it passes St Devereux, between Pontrilas and Tram Inn, en route from Newport to Hereford with the 6000 LA/MNLPS/SLOA 'Western Jubilee' rail tour on 1 October 1977. No. 6201 *Princess Elizabeth* took the train to Craven Arms, No. 6000 *King George V* then to Shrewsbury and finally No. 4498 *Sir Nigel Gresley* to Chester.

Also on 1 October 1977, the same organisers ran the 'Midland Jubilee' using the same four locos running the same stretches as the 'Western Jubilee' in the opposite direction. Here we see ex-GWR King Class 4-6-0 No. 6000 *King George V* approaching the summit of the 1 in 100 near Church Stretton. The two trips were co-ordinated for the two trains to pass at Shrewsbury.

On the final leg south of the 'Midland Jubilee' on 1 October 1977, ex-SR Merchant Navy Class 4-6-2 No. 35028 *Clan Line* is near Pandy on the 1 in 100 approach to Llanvihangel summit, north of Abergavenny. The 'Western Jubilee' had originated at Paddington and ended up at Euston; the 'Midland Jubilee' vice versa. The two trips were repeated a week later.

Ex-GWR King Class 4-6-0 No. 6000 *King George V* is storming up the 1 in 82 Gresford bank just south of Rossett on the Chester–Hereford leg of the Sussex Committee for S. R. Homes 'Southern Enterprise' on 20 May 1978. The bell presented to No. 6000 during its time with the Baltimore & Ohio Railroad in 1927 is particularly prominent in this picture.

A fleeting glimpse of sunlight highlights ex-BR Class 9F 2-10-0 *Evening Star* against the gloomy background of Pen-y-ghent as it crosses Ribblehead Viaduct on 30 September 1978 with the SLOA 'Bishop Treacy', which it hauled to Appleby. This train and 'The Lord Bishop' ran to Appleby for a memorial service held for the late Rt Revd Eric Treacy, who had sadly died of a heart attack on the station while waiting to photograph No. 92220 in May 1978.

A special event at Paddington on 1 March 1979, as ex-GWR King Class 4-6-0 No. 6000 *King George V* leaves the station with the BR Western Region '125 Anniversary of Paddington Station' run to Didcot. A large crowd is gathered on Royal Oak station to watch as it makes a parallel departure with a HST. This was the first steam-hauled train out of Paddington since 1965.

On 26 May 1979, ex-MR Compound 4-4-0 No. 1000 and ex-LNER V2 Class 2-6-2 No. 4771 *Green Arrow* are climbing the 1 in 90 near Chinley en route from Guide Bridge via Hope and Sheffield to York. The train is the SLOA 'The Curator', named in memory of the late John Scholes who had been curator of the National Railway Museum, which owned both these engines.

The tide is up at Ravenglass compared with the image on p. 49 as ex-SR MN Class 4-6-2 No. 35028 *Clan Line* departs with the BR 'Cumbrian Coast Express' bound for Sellafield from Carnforth on 28 June 1979. BR had first introduced this train in 1978, and it was repeated a number of times in 1978 and subsequent years.

Ex-LMS Jubilee Class 4-6-0 No. 5690 *Leander* is returning the BR 'Cumbrian Coast Express' from Sellafield on 28 June 1979, crossing Eskmeals Viaduct south of Ravenglass.

A locomotive combination typical of LMS Midland Main Line practice in the 1930s, ex-MR Compound 4-4-0 No. 1000 pilots ex-LMS Jubilee Class 4-6-0 No. 5690 *Leander* across Crimple Viaduct, south of Harrogate. The train is the 'Leander Enterprise' run from Derby, operated by No. 5690 from Carnforth to Leeds, where No. 1000 was attached for the run to York.

1980–89

On 22 March 1980, low early evening sunshine highlights ex-LNER A3 4-6-2 No. 4472 *Flying Scotsman* against the background of thundery clouds at Keer Holme between Wennington and Carnforth as it hauls the southern leg of the southbound SLOA 'Cumbrian Mountain Express'. This train, which first ran in January 1980, ran in two legs Carnforth to Hellifield and Hellifield to Carlisle.

Organised by SRPS Railtours on 4 May 1980, ex-NB J36 Class 0-6-0 No. 673 *Maude* worked the 'Rainhill Commemorative' rail trips between Falkirk, Edinburgh and Inverkeithing. It is somewhat dwarfed here by the surroundings as it crosses the Forth Bridge en route from Edinburgh to Inverkeithing. Built in 1891, No. 673 (65243) was named in 1919 after First World War Lieutenant General Maude.

After turning on the triangle at Inverkeithing, ex-NB J36 Class 0-6-0 No. 673 *Maude* is understandably making slow work of the 1 in 70 climb at Jamestown back onto the Forth Bridge with the SRPS rail tour on 4 May 1980. Obscured by the foliage, the road and rail links to Rosyth Docks pass under the viaduct. The SRPS saved and restored No. 65243 after it was withdrawn in 1966.

Ex-NB J36 Class 0-6-0 No. 673 *Maude* is leaving Edinburgh Waverely station on its journey back to Falkirk and Larbert with the SRPS 'Rainhill Commemorative' tour on 4 May 1980. The east signal box is artistically set in the wall and the Balmoral Hotel dominates the background.

The 'Royal Wessex' rail tour along the Cumbrian coast on 5 May 1980 was hauled from Carnforth to Sellafield by ex-MR Compound Class 4-4-0 No. 1000 and ex-LMS Jubilee Class 4-6-0 No. 5690. It is seen here passing Holme along the Kent Estuary between Arnside and Grange-over-Sands. Ex-LNER V2 No. 4771 *Green Arrow* returned the train to Carnforth.

Ex-MR Compound Class 4-4-0 No. 1000 and ex-LMS Jubilee Class 4-6-0 No. 5690 are at Lindal-in-Furness, approaching the summit of the 1 in 80 bank between Ulverston and Dalton-in-Furness on 5 May 1980. The tour was named 'The Royal Wessex' because of the intended use of ex-SR locos No. 850 *Lord Nelson* and Schools No. 925 *Cheltenham*. As can be seen, in the event there was no connection to Wessex!

An extraordinary sight at the summit of the Settle & Carlisle line on 17 May 1980 was that of ex-NB J36 Class 0-6-0 No. 673 *Maude* crossing Ais Gill Viaduct. On a perfect spring sunny day, No. 673 was making its way south from Scotland to Rainhill in Lancashire with the two preserved Caledonian Railway coaches to take part in Rocket 150.

Ex-NB J36 Class 0-6-0 No. 673 *Maude* was making very leisurely progress on its journey to Rainhill on 17 May 1980, enabling photographs at a number of locations. It is seen here at Ewood climbing from Blackburn towards Darwen. The cavalcade at Rainhill on 24–26 May was to celebrate the 150th anniversary of the trials there on the Liverpool & Manchester Railway, which featured *Rocket*.

On 15 June 1980, ex-LNER A3 Class 4-6-2 No. 4472 *Flying Scotsman* powers the SLOA 'Merseyside Express' up the 1 in 90 bank out of Chinley en route via Sheffield to York, then via Leeds and Skipton to Carnforth.

Ex-SR LN Class 4-6-0 No. 850 *Lord Nelson* is crossing Ais Gill Viaduct approaching the summit of the 1 in 100 from Ormside on the southbound run over the Settle & Carlisle line of the BR/SLOA 'Cumbrian Mountain Express' on 31 July 1980.

After a stop at Garsdale, ex-SR LN Class 4-6-0 No. 850 *Lord Nelson* continues its journey south through Dent station on 31 July 1980. Dent is the highest station in England at 1,150 feet above sea level. *Lord Nelson* was the first of sixteen locos designed by Maunsell, named after former admirals of the fleet.

The 6000 Locomotive Association 'Deeside Venturer' on 4 October 1980, starting from Taunton, was steam hauled over the Welsh Marches from Newport to Chester. Ex-GWR Hall Class 4-6-0 *Hagley Hall* powered the first leg from Newport to Hereford; it is here seen just north of Abergavenny on the 1 in 82 climb to Llanvihangel. No. 6000 *King George V* took the train on to Chester and back.

Ex-LMS Princess Royal Class 4-6-2 No. 6201 *Princess Elizabeth* is about to enter the twin-bore tunnel at Dinmore with the SLOA 'Welsh Marches Express' on 7 March 1981. Dinmore is a prominent hill around 5 miles south of Leominster. No. 6201 was built in 1933 and named after the seven-year-old girl who later became Queen Elizabeth II.

On 2 May 1981, late afternoon sunshine beautifully illuminates ex-SDJR 7F 2-8-0 No. 13809 as it makes a very smoky departure from York at Colton with the 'Pines Express' rail tour. Originating from Leicester, the train was returning to Leicester, being hauled by No. 18309 from York to Sheffield. It was the first run of this locomotive after overhaul.

On 29 July 1981, a large proportion of the UK population was watching the wedding of Prince Charles and Princess Diana. Not so those people enjoying the ride on the southbound 'Cumbrian Mountain Express', which was appropriately named the 'Wedding Belle'. It is here approaching Birkett Tunnel, south of Kirkby Stephen, hauled by ex-SR Lord Nelson Class 4-6-0 No. 850 *Lord Nelson*.

Ex-LMS Class 5MT 4-6-0 No. 5305 is reflected in the River Aire as it crosses shortly after having left Skipton with the leg to Carnforth of the SLOA 'Cumbrian Mountain Express' on 26 August 1981. This was one of the last occasions when the train ran through to Skipton, the loco changeover between the S&C and Carnforth legs was subsequently typically carried out at Hellifield.

As it crosses the River Usk, ex-GWR Hall Class 4-6-0 No. 4930 *Hagley Hall* passes the remnants of the castle when departing from Newport with the return leg of the 'Welsh Marches Pullman' on 17 October 1981. No. 4930 is owned by the Severn Valley Railway and was restored to working order in 1979.

On 3 April 1982, ex-SR King Arthur Class 4-6-0 No. 5690 *Leander* and ex-LMS 5MT Class 4-6-0 No. 5407 are near Soulby approaching Crosby Garrett on the climb from Appleby to Ais Gill with the southbound 'Cumbrian Mountain Pullman'.

On 1 May 1982, ex-LMS Class 5MT No. 5407 is at Kettlebeck between Clapham and Eldroth with the Carnforth–Hellifield portion of the SLOA 'Cumbrian Mountain Pullman'. The train was worked northbound over the S&C by No. 34092 *City of Wells*.

Ex-SR West Country Class 4-6-2 No. 34092 *City of Wells* is passing the closed Cumwhinton station on 3 May 1982 with the southbound SLOA 'Cumbrian Mountain Pullman'. The volume of steam is a perfect example of why this locomotive acquired the nickname 'Vesuvius'!

After the regular stop at Appleby, ex-SR West Country Class 4-6-2 No. 34092 *City of Wells* faced its hardest work with the 15-mile climb of mainly 1 in 100 up to Ais Gill summit. It is seen here at the summit, passing under the Garsdale–Kirkby Stephen road with Mallerstang Common in the background. Note the scorching on the front of the smokebox – a result of the hard work.

In the 1980s an additional stop was generally made at Garsdale, allowing a quick dash over what was known as the 'coal road' to Dent station, enabling a further shot of ex-SR West Country Class 4-6-2 No. 34092 *City of Wells* heading from Rise Hill Tunnel on the approach to Dent station.

Ex-SR West Country Class 4-6-2 No. 34092 *City of Wells* rounds Redness Point on the approach to Whitehaven with the return to Carnforth of the 'Cumbrian Coast Express' on 28 July 1982. The train had run from Preston and was steam hauled by No. 850 *Lord Nelson* from Carnforth to Maryport via Workington – the town that can be seen in the far background.

In Southern livery, ex-SR King Arthur Class 4-6-0 No. 777 Sir *Lamiel* is rounding the curve on the approach to Kirkham Abbey on 29 August 1982 with the return 'Scarborough Spa Express'. Organised by BR, this ran several times a week during the high summer. The River Derwent is in the background.

An integral part of the 'Scarborough Spa Express' at that time was to take in the York–Harrogate–Leeds–York loop before and after the run to Scarborough – anti-clockwise in the morning and clockwise in the evening. It is seen here passing Colton after leaving York for Leeds hauled by ex-SR 'King Arthur' Class 4-6-0 No. 777 *Sir Lamiel* on 29 August 1982.

Evening sunlight on 29 August 1982 highlights ex-SR King Arthur Class 4-6-0 *Sir Lamiel* as it crosses Bramhope Viaduct over the River Wharfe with the final leg of the 'Scarborough Spa Express' from Leeds via Harrogate to York.

Ex-LMS Jubilee Class 4-6-0 No. 5690 *Leander* has just rounded the 90-degree curve after passing the village of Armathwaite on 16 October 1982 with the Leander Locomotive/SLOA 'Leander Express', southbound over the S&C. The village is in the background over the loco.

Having moved south earlier in the year, ex-SR King Arthur Class 4-6-0 No. 777 *Sir Lamiel* is hauling the 'Welsh Marches Pullman' on 16 April 1983. It is crossing the River Usk at Penpergwm, south of Abergavenny. At the foot of the 1 in 80 down from Nantyderry, it is about to start the 6-mile climb to Llanvihangel, which steepens to 1 in 82 just beyond Abergavenny.

Having just emerged from the Severn Tunnel, ex-GWR King Class 4-6-0 *King George* V is continuing the 1 in 90 climb to Severn Tunnel Junction on 12 June 1983 with the 'Brunel Pullman' from Bristol to Newport. After turning at Newport, No. 6000 took the train on to Hereford.

On 12 June 1983, after arriving at Hereford, the 'Brunel Pullman' was taken on to Worcester by ex-LMS Class 5MT 4-6-0 No. 5000, the doyen of the class. It is here crossing the River Severn on its approach to Worcester.

Autumn tints prevail as ex-LMS Princess Coronation Class 4-6-2 *Duchess of Hamilton* rounds the curve at Armathwaite on 5 November 1983 with the southbound SLOA 'Cumbrian Mountain Express'. The poppy wreath on the front is in commemoration of Remembrance Day.

On 5 November 1983, after the regular stop at Appleby for water, No. 46229 *Duchess of Hamilton* is tackling the climb to Ais Gill after having crossed the viaduct at Smardale, north of Kirkby Stephen. No. 46229 was streamlined as built, but the casing was removed in 1947.

Ex-LMS Jubilee Class 4-6-0 No. 5690 *Leander* is passing Stokesay Castle on 28 January 1984 hauling the 'Welsh Marches Express' from Chester to Hereford. Stokesay Castle, just south of Craven Arms, is a fortified manor house built in the late thirteenth century, now an English Heritage tourist attraction.

On 18 February 1984, ex-LMS Jubilee Class 4-6-0 No. 5690 *Leander* was working south of Hereford, again with SLOA 'Welsh Marches Express' storming the summit of the 1 in 80 Goetre bank at Nant-y-derry between Abergavenny and Pontypool Road.

After turning at Newport on 18 February, No. 5690 *Leander* is heading back to Hereford, catching the late afternoon sun as it crosses the River Usk at the foot of Goetre bank south of Abergavenny. After a stint of mainline running, No. 5690 returned to its base on the SVR two days later.

The SLOA 'Cumbrian Mountain Express' on Easter weekend 1984 used an unusual combination of motive power. On 21 April, ex-SDJR 7F 2-8-0 No. 13809 is crossing the viaduct at Capernwray shortly after leaving Carnforth on the leg to Hellifield on the lower leg of the northbound run, viewed from the bank of the Lancaster Canal.

On Easter Monday 23 April 1984, having hauled the northbound leg from Hellifield to Carlisle two days earlier, ex-BR 9F 2-10-0 No. 92220 *Evening Star* is returning with the southbound 'Cumbrian Mountain Express' at Baron Wood, south of Armathwaite. A shot emerging from the tunnel has attracted a crowd of photographers.

Ex-LMS Princess Coronation Class 4-6-2 No. 46229 *Duchess of Sutherland* is at Durranhill, having just left Carlisle on the southbound SLOA 'Cumbrian Mountain Express' on 9 June 1984. The city of Carlisle is in the background. Durranhill was the site of a long-since closed Midland Railway shed.

On 9 June 1984, ex-LMS Princess Coronation Class 4-6-2 No. 46229 *Duchess of Sutherland* has emerged from Rise Hill Tunnel and is approaching Dent station with the southbound 'Cumbrian Mountain Express'. Villagers had a 5-mile walk and a climb of 1,000 feet to reach Dent station!

Ex-SR Lord Nelson Class 4-6-0 No. 850 *Lord Nelson* is at Kettlebeck between Clapham and Eldroth with the Carnforth–Hellifield portion of the northbound SLOA 'Cumbrian Mountain Pullman' on 2 July 1984. At the time of construction, the Lord Nelson Class was the most powerful locomotive in Britain.

Compared with other routes, it is unusual to see steam on the line from Newcastle to Carlisle. On 20 August 1984, ex-SR King Arthur Class 4-6-0 No. 777 *Sir Lamiel* is passing Hexham with the SLOA 'Northern Belle'. The train had run from London via Carnforth and Leeds, where No. 777 took over to work to Newcastle and then across to Carlisle.

On 20 August 1984, after a stop at Haltwhistle, No. 777 *Sir Lamiel* has just passed the village of Gilsland with the 'Northern Belle'. It is within a mile of the Roman wall here, and the Roman fort of Birdoswald is just behind the hill in the left background.

The SLOA 'Northern Belle' continued its journey south on 20 August 1984 from Carlisle on the S&C to Leeds and London. Ex-SR King Arthur Class 4-6-0 No. 777 *Sir Lamiel* was still in charge as it passed Lazonby, although it is reported that No. 777 failed shortly afterwards at Long Marton, north of Appleby.

In 1984, ex-LMS Princess Coronation Class 4-6-2 No. 46229 *Duchess of Hamilton* was one of the pool of locomotives stationed at York to power the BR-organised 'Scarborough Spa Express'. No. 46229 is at Malton on 21 August. The former streamlining can be identified by the stepped rather than curved running plate over the front bogie.

On 6 September 1984, ex-LNER A4 Class 4-6-2 No. 4498 *Sir Nigel Gresley* has passed through Rise Hill Tunnel and is approaching Dent station with the southbound SLOA 'Cumbrian Mountain Express'.

Highlighted by early autumn evening sunlight, ex-SR Merchant Navy Class 4-6-2 *Clan Line* is nearing the summit of the 1 in 80 bank from Abergavenny at Llanvihangel Crucorney on 20 October 1984 with the return leg of the 'Welsh Marches Express' from Newport to Hereford.

With the swirling River Wye in the foreground and autumn tints in the Eign district behind, ex-GWR King Class 4-6-0 *King George V* leaves Hereford for Newport with a 'Welsh Marches Express' on 3 November 1984.

On 3 November 1984, ex-GWR King Class 4-6-0 No. 6000 *King George V* is at Llanvihangel Crucorney with the southbound 'Welsh Marches Express' heading for Newport. The hill in the background is on the edge of the Brecon Beacons National Park.

The SLOA 'Welsh Marches Express' departs Newport and crosses the River Usk en route to Hereford hauled by ex-GWR Modified Hall Class 4-6-0 No. 6960 *Raveningham Hall*. Newport is well known for its transporter bridge over the Usk, which can be seen in the background to the right. Raveningham Hall is a stately home near Norwich in Norfolk – hardly GWR territory!

Ex-GWR Hall Class 4-6-0 No. 4930 *Hagley Hall* is crossing the viaduct at Frampton Mansell with the Pullman Rail 'Red Dragon' on 2 February 1985. It is on the 1 in 60 approaching Sapperton Tunnel heading for Swindon on the line from Gloucester and Stroud. Hagley Hall is a Grade I listed eighteenth-century house in Worcestershire.

The year 1985 was the 150th anniversary of the Great Western Railway, and the first of many events was the first GWR steam-hauled train to the West Country for over thirty years. Ex-GWR 4-6-0s No. 4930 *Hagley Hall* and No. 7819 *Hinton Manor* are seen running alongside the River Teign on the approach to Teignmouth with SLOA 'Great Western Limited' from Plymouth to Bristol on 8 April.

On 6 July 1985, ex-GWR Hall Class 4-6-0 No. 4930 *Hagley Hall* and ex-BR Castle Class 4-6-0 No. 7029 *Clun Castle* are leaving Newport heading for Cardiff with the Pullman Rail 'Western Stalwart'. The pair had picked up the train from London at Kidderminster and would work it back to Hereford.

During the late summer BR organised a number of GWR steam-hauled celebration excursions between Swindon and Gloucester using a pool of locomotives. On 25 August, ex-GWR King Class 4-6-0 No. 6000 *King George V* is running down the 1 in 60 over Frampton Mansell Viaduct heading for Gloucester.

The SLOA 'Great Western Limited' ran from Paddington to Plymouth and back on 1 September 1985. It was hauled from Plymouth to Bristol by ex-GWR Castle Class 4-6-0s No. 5051 *Drysllwyn Castle* and No. 7029 *Clun Castle*, seen here at Cogload Junction having left Taunton. It is here that the lines to Bristol and Newbury diverge.

On 6 September 1985 Cornwall saw its first steam loco since 1964. On this date, BR ran a 'GW150 Celebration Tour' from Plymouth to Truro with ex-BR Castle Class 4-6-0 No. 7029 *Clun Castle*. It is seen here returning from Truro, crossing Combe St Stephens Viaduct 5 miles before St Austell. Four ivy-covered piers from the original Brunel viaduct, which was replaced in 1886, can be seen alongside.

After a stop at Lostwithiel on 6 September 1985, ex-BR Castle Class 4-6-0 No. 7029 *Clun Castle* is passing Liskeard with the return BR excursion from Truro to Plymouth. With no turning facilities at Truro, No. 7029 was turned at Par on the outward journey and worked the train tender-first from there to Truro.

Two days later, on 8 September, ex-BR/GWR Castle Class 4-6-0s No. 7029 *Clun Castle* and No. 5051 *Drysllwyn Castle* hauled a 'GW150 Celebration Tour' from Plymouth to Bristol. It is seen here near Willand having just passed Cullompton, between Exeter and Taunton.

The inaugural mainline steam run of ex-GWR City Class 4-4-0 No. 3440 *City of Truro* after restoration on the Severn Valley Railway took place on 20 October 1985. It is seen here crossing the River Severn shortly after leaving Gloucester with a return trip to Gloucester. The scene is not enhanced by the choice of carriage stock!

Shortly after departing from a stop at Lydney, ex-GWR City Class 4-4-0 No. 3440 *City of Truro* is heading towards Newport with its inaugural run after restoration. This return run from Gloucester to Newport was billed as a 'mystery tour'; it was supposedly clouded in secrecy, yet everyone knew the details well in advance!

A 'Welsh Marches Express' with a bit of a difference! Probably the one and only time that ex-GWR City Class 4-4-0 No. 3440 *City of Truro* and ex-GWR King Class 4-6-0 No. 6000 *King George V* have run in tandem as they climb the 1 in 82 between Onibury and Craven Arms on the way from Hereford to Shrewsbury on 24 May 1986.

Viewed from almost the same spot, ex-GWR City Class 4-4-0 No. 3440 *City of Truro* and ex-GWR King Class 4-6-0 No. 6000 *King George V* return from Shrewsbury on 24 May 1986. Skokesay Castle is prominent in the background. No. 3440's fame comes from a reported speed of 102.3 mph down Wellington bank on 9 May 1904, a claim that has been disputed ever since.

The evening sunlight against a stormy background highlights ex-LMS Jubilee Class 4-6-0 No. 5593 *Kolhapur* as it rounds the curve at Bearley Junction shortly after leaving Stratford-upon-Avon with the return 'Shakespeare Express' on 7 June 1986. The view is from the aqueduct carrying the Stratford-upon-Avon canal.

On 4 July 1987, ex-GWR King Class 4-6-0 No. 6000 *King George V* is crossing the River Dee shortly after leaving Chester with the return to Hereford of the 'Diamond Jubilee Express', organised by the 6000 Locomotive Association to mark the 60th anniversary of the loco. The line carries both the Welsh Marches and North Wales Coast routes, but rationalisation has deemed four tracks unnecessary.

In the summer of 1987, ex-GWR Manor Class 4-6-0 No. 7819 *Hinton Manor* was based at Machynlleth to run a number of BR-organised 'Cardigan Bay Express' trips between there and Aberystwyth and Barmouth. On 16 August, No. 7819 is crossing the Grade II* listed Barmouth Bridge across the Mawddach Estuary. Cadair Idris is in the background to the left.

During September 1987 a number of return trips were organised between Swansea and Carmarthen. On 19 September, the first of two return trips of the Pembrey Travel 'Carmarthen Express' was hauled by ex-GWR King Class 4-6-0 No. 6000 *King George V*, here returning just past Kidwelly. No. 6000 had its last run a week later and is now on static exhibition.

The second return run of the 'Carmarthen Express' on 19 September was carried out by ex-BR Castle Class 4-6-0 No. 7029 *Clun Castle*. As viewed from the foreshore, early evening sunlight catches the train as it rounds the headland of the Tywi Estuary at St Ishmael.

In 1988, ex-LNER A4 Class 4-6-2 No. 4468 *Mallard* hauled a number of rail tours to commemorate the 50th anniversary of its 126-mph record run on 3 July 1938. The very last of these runs was on 27 August, when it hauled a circular trip from York via Newcastle and Carlisle. It is seen here near Haltwhistle, between Hexham and Carlisle.

The BR-organised last run of ex-LNER A4 Class 4-6-2 No. 4468 *Mallard* continued from Carlisle over the S&C via Skipton to Leeds and York. It is seen at Birkett Common, just beyond Kirkby Stephen. It is evident from the smoke trail that it is moving slowly; in fact, No. 4468 stopped for a 'blow up' a few yards further on, with the last coach roughly where the loco is in this picture.

On 29 October 1988, ex-LMS Class 8F No. 48151 is crossing the River Ribble at Sheriff Brow just south of Helwith Bridge with the Flying Scotsman Services northbound 'Cumbrian Mountain Express'. It actually took around 7 minutes for the train to reach this point from the tree-lined cutting at Stainforth (seen in the distance) due to much slipping caused by wet leaves on the line.

Ex-SR Merchant Navy Class 4-6-2 No. 35028 *Clan Line* passes immediately in front of Conwy Castle, completed in 1287, as it heads towards Holyhead with the InterCity Charter Train Unit 'North Wales Coast Express' on 1 August 1989. There is the apocryphal story of an overseas visitor having remarked 'fancy building a castle so close to the railway'.

On 30 September 1989, ex-LNER V2 Class 2-6-0 No. 4771 *Green Arrow* is passing through Baron Wood between Armathwaite and Lazonby with the southbound BR 'Cumbrian Mountain Express'. Built in 1936, No. 4771 was named after the railway express freight service.